ECUADOR

Michelle Lomberg

AV2

www.openlightbox.com

AV2

CONTENTS

AV2 is optimized for use on any device

Your interactive eBook comes with...

Contents
Browse a live contents page to easily navigate through resources

Audio
Listen to sections of the book read aloud

Videos
Watch informative video clips

Weblinks
Gain additional information for research

Slideshows
View images and captions

Try This!
Complete activities and hands-on experiments

Key Words
Study vocabulary, and complete a matching word activity

Quizzes
Test your knowledge

Share
Share titles within your Learning Management System (LMS) or Library Circulation System

Citation
Create bibliographical references following APA, CMOS, and MLA styles

This title is part of our AV2 digital subscription

1-Year 3–8 Subscription
ISBN 978-1-7911-3306-1

Access hundreds of AV2 titles with our digital subscription.
Sign up for a FREE trial at **www.openlightbox.com/trial**

The digital components of this book are guaranteed to stay active for at least five years from the date of publication.

Ecuador

CONTENTS

Ecuador Overview

Ecuador is located on the northwestern coast of the continent of South America. The **equator** extends east–west through northern Ecuador, giving the country its name. Once part of the **Inca Empire**, Ecuador was later **colonized** by Spain. Today, this independent country has a rich history and diverse population. Its economy depends on manufacturing, farming, and tourism. Many people visit Ecuador's Galápagos Islands to see the area's unusual plants and animals. In fact, the British scientist Charles Darwin formed his theory of **natural selection** in the 19th century after visiting there. Ecuador's varied landscapes also include beaches, active volcanoes, and thick rainforests.

Ecuadorian dancers

Ecuador is the only South American country that uses the **U.S. dollar** as its **official currency**.

About **16 percent** of the world's bird species can be found in Ecuador.

Ecuador is the world's largest exporter of bananas, with sales of approximately **$3.8 billion**.

Ecuador is home to approximately 2,000 jaguars. Most live in the country's rainforests.

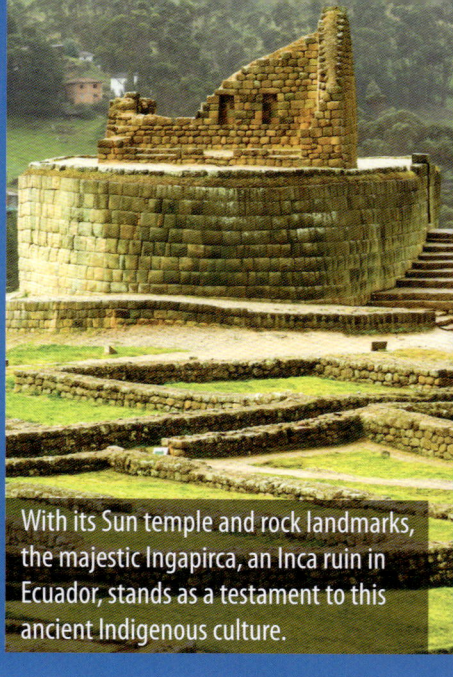

With its Sun temple and rock landmarks, the majestic Ingapirca, an Inca ruin in Ecuador, stands as a testament to this ancient Indigenous culture.

More than 10 waterfalls, including the El Pailón del Diablo, can be seen on the Ruta de las Cascadas, a 37-mile (60-kilometer) trail in central Ecuador.

Street parades, music, and dance are a big part of the many Ecuadorian festivals held throughout the year.

Ecuardor's street markets sell colorful rugs and other Indigenous handicrafts.

Hornado is a traditional Ecuadorian dish consisting of marinated pork that has been cooked in a wood-burning clay oven.

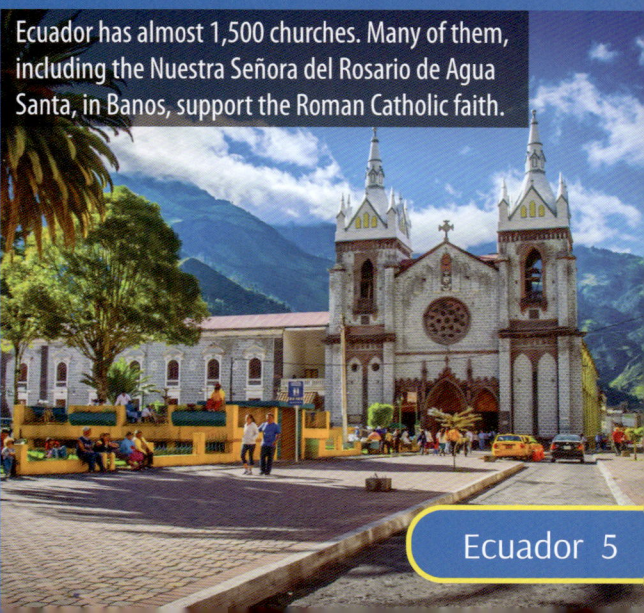

Ecuador has almost 1,500 churches. Many of them, including the Nuestra Señora del Rosario de Agua Santa, in Banos, support the Roman Catholic faith.

Exploring Ecuador

Ecuador covers an area of 109,484 square miles (283,562 square kilometers). The country is bordered by Colombia to the north and Peru to the east and south. The Pacific Ocean forms its western border. Ecuador is the smallest of the Andean countries, which also include Bolivia, Colombia, and Peru. The Andes Mountains, which extend north–south in western South America, cover much of these four countries. Ecuador's major rivers include the Guayas and the Putumayo.

A Cotopaxi

One of the world's most active volcanoes, Cotopaxi rises to a height of 19,393 feet (5,911 meters). This volcano has erupted more than 85 times since 1744. Its most recent eruption occurred in 2022. When conditions are safe, however, it is a popular mountain for hikers.

B Quito

Quito is the capital of Ecuador. Founded by the Spanish in 1534, the city has a mixture of European and Indigenous **architectural** styles.

C Cuicocha Lake

Cuicocha is one of many volcanic crater lakes in the region north of Quito. Such lakes form in the bowl-shaped tops, or craters, of volcanoes. Cuicocha is 2 miles (3 km) across and 600 feet (180 m) deep.

D Putumayo River

The Putumayo River begins in the Andes and flows east for 1,000 miles (1,600 km). The river forms part of Ecuador's border with Colombia. It empties into the Amazon River.

Map of Ecuador

PACIFIC OCEAN

CUICOCHA LAKE **C**

QUITO **B**

A COTOPAXI

D

PUTUMAYO RIVER

E c u a d o r

Legend

Ecuador Land River

Water Capital City

N

SCALE

100 km

100 miles

Land and Climate

Amazon Rainforest

Ecuador's geography is varied. The Andes Mountains and the Amazon Rainforest cover much of the country. A boundary, or fault, between two of Earth's **tectonic plates** lies off Ecuador's coast. The movement of these plates and activity within Earth below the fault cause Ecuador to have many earthquakes and volcanoes.

Ecuador has four distinct geographic regions. The Costa region lies along the Pacific coast. It is mainly flat with beaches along the shore, **plains**, and forests. The Costa has a warm and humid climate. Its heaviest rainfall occurs between December and May.

Chimborazo rises to a height of 20,702 feet (6,310 m) above sea level. Its most recent eruption was in 550 AD.

Summits Farthest from Earth's Core

Chimborazo Ecuador	Huascarán Peru	Yerupajá Peru
①	②	③
3,967.1 miles (6,384.4 km)	3967.1 miles (6,384.4 km)	3,967.0 miles (6,384.3 km)

The Sierra region covers the part of the Andes in Ecuador. This region includes two lines of mountains that run north–south. They are known as the western chain and the eastern chain.

Between the mountain chains lies a valley called the Avenue of the Volcanoes that stretches for 200 miles (322 km). This valley features active and **dormant** volcanoes, including Chimborazo, Ecuador's highest mountain. Beneath the often snow-covered mountain peaks, the valley has mild temperatures year round.

Ecuador's coastline extends for 1,390 miles (2,237 km).

East of the Sierra lies the Oriente region. This area makes up about half of Ecuador's land. Most of the region is part of the Amazon Rainforest. The weather is hot and humid year-round, with frequent rainfall. The Oriente region includes some of the wettest parts of Ecuador.

The Galápagos Islands are in the Pacific Ocean about 600 miles (965 km) from Ecuador's coast. This archipelago, or group of islands, includes 13 large islands and 7 smaller ones. Each was formed by eruptions of underwater volcanoes. Cool ocean currents keep temperatures moderate. The islands receive little rainfall.

The Galápagos Islands are known for their unique landscapes, ranging from arid deserts to dense forests.

Plants and Animals

Mangroves in northern Ecuador

Many types of plants flourish in Ecuador. **Mangroves** grow along the shore in the Costa region. The mountains of the Sierra are home to evergreen trees, small plants, and tough grasses. Misty **cloud forests** hold and create moisture to water orchids, ferns, and mosses. In the Oriente region, tall trees such as the kapok form the canopy, or top layer of branches in a forest. Vines, ferns, orchids, and other tropical plants thrive beneath. The Galápagos Islands have about 600 plant species. They include mangroves, morning glory vines, and candelabra cactuses.

Animals, too, are part of Ecuador's extensive **biodiversity**. Ecuador has more bird species than the entire continent of North America. Andean foxes and deer roam the mountains, while Andean condors fly overhead. Anacondas, otters, and jaguars live in the rainforest. The Galápagos Islands are home to their own tortoise, cormorant, and fur seal species. More than 12 percent of the world's bat species live in Ecuador.

The world's largest living tortoise, the Galápagos giant tortoise, can be more than 4 feet (1.2 m) long and weigh more than 650 pounds (295 kilograms).

Natural Resources

Trans-Ecuadorian System Oil Pipeline (SOTE)

One of Ecuador's most important natural resources is petroleum, or oil. Most of the country's oil comes from the Oriente region. Ecuador's two oil companies, Petroecuador and Petroamazonas, are run by the government. The oil they produce helps meet the country's energy needs. In addition, much of it is sold internationally, bringing money into the country. Ecuador's rivers also produce energy. The country has spent billions of dollars to develop **hydroelectricity** projects.

Ecuador's coastal waters are full of another natural resource, fish. The cold, slow-moving water along South America's Pacific coast is called the Humboldt, or Peru, Current. It supports many types of fish, including sardines and an anchovy species called anchoveta. Ecuador is the leading producer of shrimp in the Americas. Canned tuna is also a major export.

Metals such as gold and silver are mined in Ecuador. Timber is also an important natural resource. Balsa, teak, and pine are harvested from Ecuador's forests and used to make plywood and furniture.

On average, Ecuador catches about 300,000 tons (272,155 metric tons) of tuna every year. This is more than any other country fishing in the eastern Pacific Ocean.

Tourism

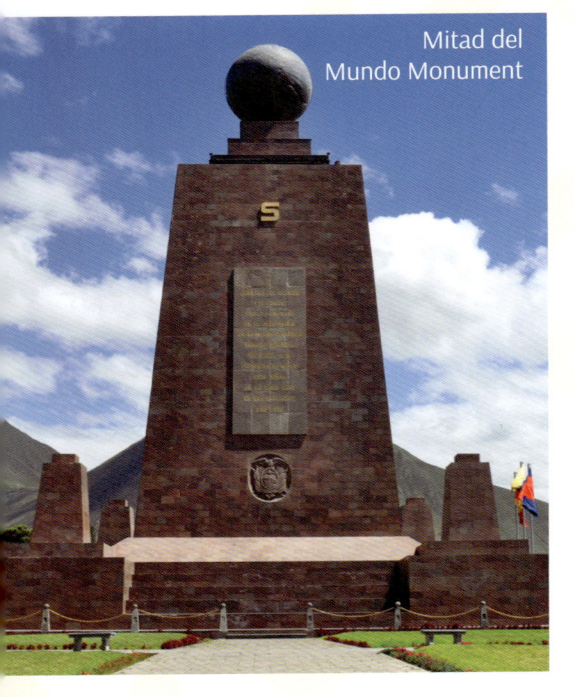

Mitad del Mundo Monument

More than 1.4 million tourists from around the world come to Ecuador each year. They visit the country's centuries-old cities and colonial buildings. Ecuador's natural areas are also appealing tourist destinations.

Many people visit Quito, the oldest capital city in South America. This historic city is one of Ecuador's five **UNESCO** World Heritage Sites. The churches of San Francisco and Santo Domingo are examples of the **Baroque** architecture that is common in Quito.

North of Quito is the popular landmark called *Mitad del Mundo*, or "Middle of the Earth" in Spanish. It features an equator monument and a yellow line, where visitors imagine they are straddling two hemispheres. However, in fact, this tourist attraction is about 820 feet (250 m) from the true equator.

The **Galápagos Marine Reserve** was established in 1998.

Almost **3,000 marine species** can be found within the Galápagos Marine Reserve.

The Galápagos Marine Reserve covers an area of **76,448 square miles** (198,000 sq. km).

Marine iguanas are one of the many creatures that scuba divers can see up close in the Galápagos Marine Reserve.

Many tourists also visit Cuenca. In 1557, the Spanish founded this beautiful city, whose full name is Santa Ana de los Ríos de Cuenca. The bright, sunny streets of Cuenca's historic city center feature large cathedrals and well-preserved colonial homes.

Adventure seekers come to the volcanoes and mountains of the Sierra. It is Ecuador's most popular tourist region. People climb, ski, hike, and mountain bike. They also relax in the region's hot springs.

Cathedral of the Immaculate Conception, Cuenca

The Oriente offers tourists a chance to see the Amazon Rainforest's biodiversity. Visitors to Yasuní National Park hike jungle trails and climb above the forest canopy. Birdwatchers can observe more than 650 species of birds.

Visitors to the Costa region can relax on Ecuador's many beaches. Diving, whale watching, and snorkeling are also popular activities on the country's Pacific coast. After a day in the surf, tourists can enjoy fresh seafood in one of the area's many restaurants.

The Galápagos Islands are another UNESCO World Heritage Site. Visitors see plants and animals found nowhere else on Earth. At the Galápagos Marine Reserve, tourists swim with dolphins, whale sharks, and sea lions.

Visitors to Yasuní National Park can travel the rivers of the Amazon River Basin on a guided canoe tour.

Industry

Manufacturing is a growing industry in Ecuador. Many factories build automobiles. Kia and Hyundai assemble vehicles for sale within Ecuador and throughout South America and Central America.

People in Ecuador have made **textiles** since ancient times. Today, the country produces spun yarn and fabrics, as well as finished clothing. Ecuador exports textiles to neighboring countries and around the world. Atuntaqui, in the northern Sierra region, is a textile-production center.

Agriculture employs more than one-fourth of Ecuador's workers. The country's largest agricultural export is bananas. Other leading exports include palm oil, coffee, and cacao beans, which are used to make chocolate. Farmers in Ecuador also grow flowers, including roses, for export. Rice and barley crops are eaten mostly within the country. Fish farming is another profitable industry in Ecuador. Fish farmers raise fish for food in tanks or contained ponds.

Ecuador is South America's third-largest producer of quinoa, after Bolivia and Peru. Most of the country's quinoa crops are grown in the Andes by the area's Indigenous groups.

Goods and Services

Service industries employ more than one-half of Ecuador's workers. People in these industries provide services instead of producing goods. Tour guides, chefs, bus drivers, doctors, teachers, and government employees are examples of service workers. Some people with service jobs are informal laborers. These workers have jobs that often do not follow the government's labor laws.

Hotel front desk agent

Ecuador trades with nations in all parts of the world. The United States is Ecuador's biggest trading partner. About 26 percent of Ecuador's **imports** come from the United States, followed by 23 percent from China and 6 percent from Colombia. Ecuador exports more goods to the United States than to any other country. After the United States, the countries that are the largest buyers of Ecuadoran products are China, Panama, Chile, and Colombia.

The Port of Guayaquil is Ecuador's largest shipping port. Approximately 93 percent of all sea containers arriving in or leaving the country do so through this port.

Indigenous Peoples

Indigenous peoples have lived in today's Ecuador for thousands of years. **Archaeological** evidence shows that humans may have been in the area since 10,000 BC. They survived by hunting and by gathering plant foods. Farming began centuries later. Communities were growing corn in the Costa region by about 4,500 BC. Various tribes joined to form the Kingdom of Quito in about 1,000 AD. This kingdom lasted for several hundred years.

Ceramic figurine from Bahia people of Ecuador's central coast, 4th to 7th century

In 1463, the Inca began moving from what is now Peru north into the Ecuador region. By the end of the 15th century, Ecuador was under Incan control. Inca society flourished in the Andes. The Inca Empire had advanced architecture, engineering, and farming methods. The Inca also brought the Quechua language to the area.

Cuenca is home to the remains of an Inca city called Tomebamba. At one time, Tomebamba served as the administrative center for the northern part of Inca Empire.

Today, Ecuador is home to at least 14 Indigenous groups. Many of these groups continue their traditional ways of life. Most Indigenous people in Ecuador still speak Quechua.

The Age of Exploration

In European history, the Age of Exploration refers to the period between the 15th and 17th centuries when explorers searched for new trade routes to Asia and new sources of wealth for European nations. In 1492, Spain sent Italian navigator Christopher Columbus across the Atlantic Ocean to find a route to Asia. Instead, he reached the Caribbean and founded a colony on the island of Hispaniola. A Spanish explorer named Francisco Pizarro arrived there in 1502.

Pizarro began his exploration of Central and South America with trips from Hispaniola to present-day Panama and Colombia. In 1523, he sailed down Colombia's Pacific coast. On his next voyage, between 1526 and 1528, Pizarro sailed farther south, along the coast of Ecuador.

Pizarro returned to Ecuador in 1532. His goal was to reach Peru and the center of the rich Inca Empire. In 1533, Pizarro and his men seized the Incan capital city of Cuzco, in Peru.

When Pizarro arrived in Ecuador in 1532, he was accompanied by only 180 soldiers. Even with such a small contingent, he was able to advance quickly through the land and gain control of an empire that had a population of about 5 million.

Early Settlers

By 1534, Spain had completed its conquest of the Inca Empire and gained control of today's Ecuador. Under Spanish rule, the Ecuador region was included in larger colonies. In 1740, it became part of the **viceroyalty** of New Granada. New Granada included present-day Colombia, Panama, Venezuela, and Ecuador.

Andrés Hurtado de Mendoza of Spain led the viceroyalty of Peru, which contained Ecuador, from 1555 until his death in 1561.

Spanish settlers brought their language and Roman Catholic religion to the region. They built churches and **monasteries** in the style that was common in 16th-century Spain. Spanish settlers were given land with control over everyone who lived on it. Under Spanish rule, Ecuador's Indigenous peoples were forced to pay taxes, work for free, and become Christians.

Spain also brought enslaved people from Africa to Ecuador. These people labored mainly on **plantations**. Slavery was outlawed when Ecuador became independent in the 1800s. On July 9, 1816, leaders from all parts of the former viceroyalty met in Argentina. They declared the region independent from Spain and set up the United Provinces of the Río de la Plata. Buenos Aires was the capital of the Argentine section, while Uruguay, Paraguay, and Bolivia created their own governments.

La Balbanera chapel, originally built by the Spanish in 1534, is one of the oldest churches in Ecuador. However, much of it had to be rebuilt after an earthquake in 1797.

Most Spanish settlers lived in the Sierra region. Ecuador was not as rich in gold as other parts of the former Inca Empire. Therefore, Spanish settlers in Ecuador had built an economy based largely on agriculture and textiles. They grew crops and raised livestock for both food and for the raw materials needed to make fabrics. Indigenous people worked as **serfs** on ranches or plantations and in textile mills.

Ecuador's Indigenous peoples fought Spanish efforts to control them and their land. Spanish colonization was least successful in the Oriente region. In 1599, the Shuar people drove the Spanish from their territory.

In the early 1800s, South American military leader Simón Bolívar led revolts against Spanish rule in New Granada. In 1822, Bolívar and his ally Antonio José de Sucre helped Ecuadoran rebels win independence from Spain. By then, other parts of New Granada had already gained independence and become the **republic** of Gran Colombia. Ecuador joined Gran Colombia for a time but declared itself an independent republic with its own **constitution** in 1830.

On May 24, 1822, Antonio José de Sucre and his army won an important victory over Spanish forces at the Battle of Pichincha. Under the terms of the official surrender, the nearby city of Quito was liberated, along with several Ecuadorian provinces.

Population

About 18 million people live in Ecuador, and the population is growing by close to 1 percent each year. The country's population density is 191 people per square mile (74 per sq. km). Ecuador has more residents per square mile (sq. km) than many other countries. The population density in the United States is 98 people per square mile (38 per sq. km).

Almost two-thirds of Ecuador's people live in **urban** areas. The city of Quito is home to more than 1.9 million people. Ecuador's largest city, Guayaquil, has approximately 3.2 million residents. The majority of Ecuador's people live in the Sierra and Costa regions. The Galápagos Islands and rainforest areas in Oriente are the regions of the country with the fewest people.

Ecuador's population is young. Approximately 27 percent of Ecuadorians are under the age of 15, compared to only about 18 percent in the United States. The average Ecuadoran can expect to live to 76.8 years old, slightly lower than the figure of 80.9 years for the United States. The average Ecuadoran student leaves school at age 16. However, the country's **literacy rate** is 93.9 percent.

Guayaquil's Malecon 2000 promenade

Politics and Government

The government of Ecuador is based on the country's current constitution, which was passed in 2008. There are three branches of government. They are the executive, legislative, and judicial branches. The National Assembly is the legislative branch of the government. It passes laws and appoints Constitutional Court judges. The president and **cabinet** are the highest officials in the executive branch of the government. They enforce laws passed by the National Assembly. Ecuador's judicial branch includes the National Court of Justice and the Constitutional Court.

Danial Noboa, Ecuador's 48th president

Ecuador's citizens vote for the president, vice president, and members of the National Assembly. All serve four-year terms. In the past, presidents were limited to two terms. However, recent changes to the constitution allow the president to be reelected an unlimited number of times.

The offices of Ecuador's executive branch are housed in the Carondelet Palace, in Quito.

Cultural Groups

Many different groups have contributed to Ecuador's culture. They include Indigenous peoples, settlers from Europe, and enslaved people from Africa. Today, more than 77 percent of the population is mestizo, or people with both European and Indigenous origins. The rest of the population is made up of people whose origins are Montubio, Indigenous, European, or African. Montubio people have a mixture of European, African, and coastal Indigenous heritage.

Ecuador's Indigenous peoples include the Quechua, the Shuar, and the Huaorani. Like the Inca before them, many Quechua people are farmers. They grow corn and potatoes in Ecuador's valleys and highlands. The Shuar people live in hills and rainforests of the Oriente. Their traditional way of life involves farming and hunting.

Ecuador's Huaorani people also hunt and gather food to survive. However, some now work in the lumber industry. In the past, the Huaorani have preferred to remain separate from Europeans and even from other Indigenous peoples.

Almost **99 percent** of Ecuadorians speak Spanish.

Protestantism is the second-most common religion in Ecuador, with about **11 percent** practicing it.

Altogether, Ecuador's Indigenous population is about **1.1 million**.

Killa Raymi, or "Festival of the Moon" in the Quechua language, is an ancient spiritual ceremony held in the Andes of Ecuador and Peru. The celebration includes dancing and colorful costumes.

Spanish is Ecuador's official language. The two main Indigenous languages are Quechua and Shuar. They are official languages of relations between cultures. This means that their use is not limited to the people who speak them as their first language. Other Indigenous languages are official only in the areas where they are spoken.

Native Quechua teacher and students

More than two-thirds of Ecuador's people are Roman Catholic. Some Indigenous Ecuadorians practice their traditional beliefs. Others follow a combination of traditional Indigenous beliefs and Roman Catholicism.

Some Ecuadorians express their culture through distinctive regional dress. The Otavaleño people of northern Ecuador have been skilled weavers since before Inca times. They often dress in traditional clothes. Otavaleño women wear blue skirts, white blouses, and shawls. The men wear blue ponchos, short white trousers, and felt hats.

Ecuadoran food is another sign of the country's cultural diversity, and popular dishes often vary by region. People on the coast enjoy seafood dishes such as *encocado de camarones*, or prawns in coconut sauce. In the Sierra region, people dine on *cuy*, which is roasted guinea pig.

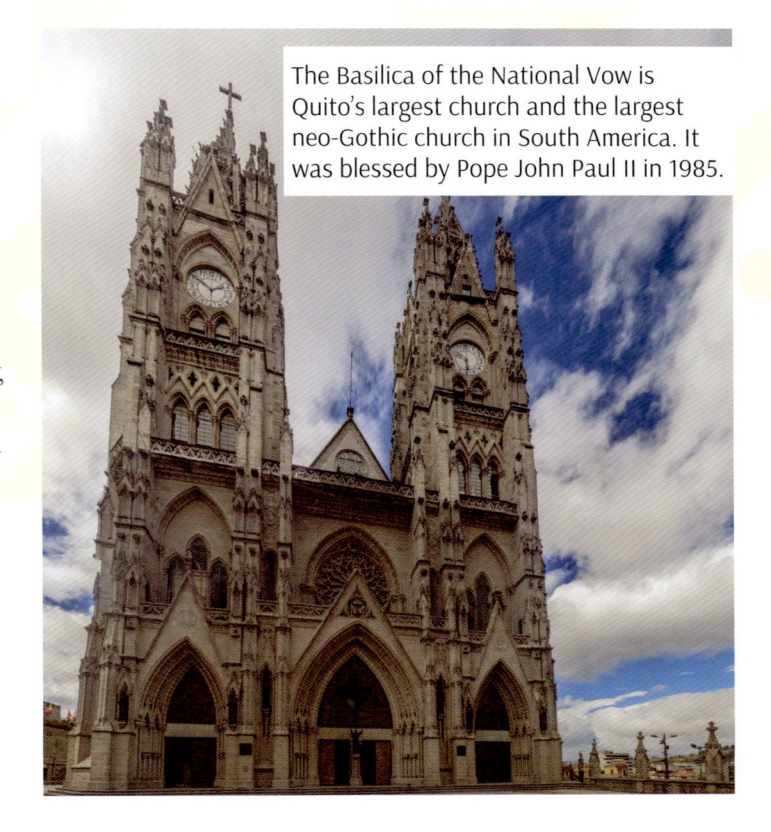
The Basilica of the National Vow is Quito's largest church and the largest neo-Gothic church in South America. It was blessed by Pope John Paul II in 1985.

Arts and Entertainment

Making a Panama hat

The arts help to both unify Ecuadorians and celebrate their diversity. Visual and performing arts are a large part of the culture. *La Casa de la Cultura Ecuatoriana*, or the House of Ecuadoran Culture," in Quito was founded in 1944. The organization promotes the country's cultural heritage as well as art events.

Traditional arts and crafts are popular in Ecuador. Fiber arts include cloth weaving and hat making. Artists use local materials such as alpaca yarn from the Sierra and palm plants from the area around Guayaquil. Panama hats are an example of a craft tradition that originated in Ecuador. Today, they are woven by hand at Montecristi.

Ecuadoran artists express themselves using traditional European art forms, too. The paintings and sculptures of Oswaldo Guayasamín appear in galleries around the world. His art focuses on themes of peace and social justice.

Traditional music in Ecuador draws on Indigenous, Spanish, and African traditions. The Indigenous music of the Andes typically features the flute and *rondador*, a **panpipe** made of reeds. *Pasillo* music resembles the European waltz. In *pasillo* songs, guitars and flutes accompany poetic lyrics.

Ecuadorian boy playing rondador

Marimba music is popular in the Costa region. The origins of this music can be traced to West Africa. Marimba is the name of both the music and the instrument on which it is played. The instrument is a set of wooden bars that are struck with mallets, much as a xylophone is played.

Other types of music are also popular in Ecuador. Singer Mirella Cesa has developed a style of Andean popular music called andipop. Nicolá Cruz blends traditional Andean music with modern techno beats. This style is known as Andes step.

Mirella Cesa is often referred to as the "mother of andipop" for her contributions to the genre.

Sports

Alberto Spencer

Ecuadorians consider *fútbol*, or soccer, their national sport. In 2007, the national men's team won gold at the Pan American Games. The team has qualified for the FIFA World Cup four times, most recently in 2022. The national women's team has had international success as well. In 2006, it qualified for the Pan American Games. In 2015, Ecuador sent a team to the women's World Cup tournament for the first time.

One of South America's greatest soccer players was the Ecuadorian Alberto Spencer. Known as *cabeza mágica*, or "magic head," for his skill at heading the ball, Spencer scored a career total of 451 goals. His talent took him from Ecuador to play in Uruguay and Spain in the 1960s and early 1970s.

Ecuador made its first-ever appearance at the FIFA U-17 Women's World Cup in 2024, where it advanced to the quarterfinals.

Brian Pintado at the 2024 Paris Olympics

Basketball is another popular team sport in Ecuador. Students play on high school and college teams. In 2015, the country took part in its first FIBA Americas Women's Championship.

Ecuador has won 10 Olympic medals. Its best showing took place at the 2024 Paris Olympics, when it won five. This included Brian Pintado's gold in the Men's 20-kilometer Race Walk, a long-distance competition that requires one foot to be on the ground at all times.

Ecuador also has its own sports. Ecuavoley, a game that may date back to before colonial times, is similar to volleyball. Teams of three players hit or throw a ball across a high net. *Pelota de guante* is another sport with Indigenous origins. This racquet sport was traditionally played with heavy spiked discs. A modern version, called *pelota nacional* or *chaza*, is still played today.

Equavoley game

Activity
Mapping Ecuador

We use many tools to interpret maps and to understand the locations of features such as cities, states, lakes, and rivers. The map on the following page has many tools to help interpret information on the map of Ecuador.

Mapping Tools

The compass rose shows north, south, east, and west. The points in between represent northeast, northwest, southeast, and southwest.

The map scale shows that the distances on a map represent much longer distances in real life. If you measure the distance between objects on a map, you can use the map scale to calculate the actual distance in miles or kilometers between those two points.

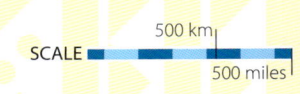

The lines of latitude and longitude are long lines that appear on maps. The lines of latitude run east to west and measure how far north or south of the equator a place is located. The lines of longitude run north to south and measure how far east or west of the Prime Meridian a place is located. A location on a map can be found by using the two numbers where latitude and longitude meet. This number is called a coordinate and is written using degrees and direction. For example, the city of Quito would be found at 0.2°S and 78°W on a map.

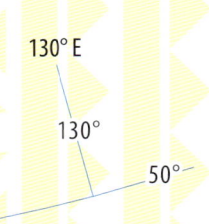

Using the map and the appropriate tools, complete the activities below.

Locating with latitude and longitude
1. Which city is located at 3°S and 79°W?
2. Which mountain is located at 1.5°S and 79°W?
3. Which volcanic peak is found at 1°S and 78°W?

Distances between points
4. Using the map scale and a ruler, calculate the approximate distance between Quito and Cuenca.
5. Using the map scale and a ruler, calculate the approximate distance between Quito and Guayaquil.
6. Using the map scale and a ruler, calculate the approximate distance between Guayaquil and Cuenca.

ANSWERS 1. Cuenca 2. Chimborazo 3. Cotopaxi 4. 190 miles (300 km) 5. 170 miles (270 km) 6. 80 miles (130 km)

Map of Ecuador

Pacific Ocean

80° 78° 76°

0° 0°

★ Quito
▲ Cotopaxi

▲ Mount Chimborazo

2° 2°

● Guayaquil

● Cuenca

4° 4°

80° 78° 76°

Legend

★ Capital City   ● City   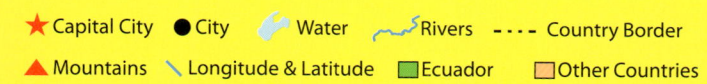 Water   Rivers   - - - - Country Border

▲ Mountains   Longitude & Latitude   ▢ Ecuador   ▢ Other Countries

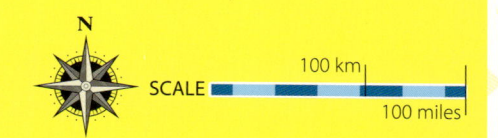

N

SCALE   100 km   100 miles

Quiz

1 What is the capital of Ecuador?

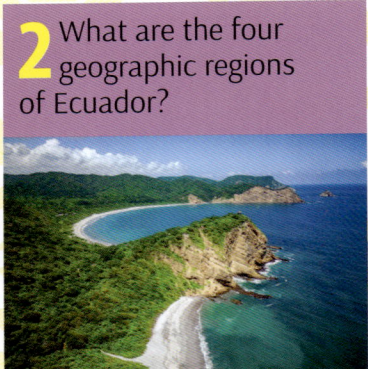

2 What are the four geographic regions of Ecuador?

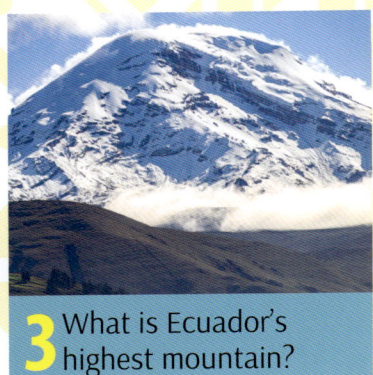

3 What is Ecuador's highest mountain?

4 Which product is Ecuador's largest agricultural export?

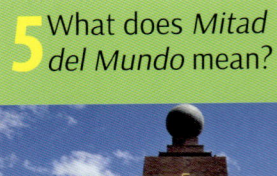

5 What does *Mitad del Mundo* mean?

6 How many Indigenous groups live in Ecuador today?

7 In what year did Ecuador declare itself an independent republic?

8 What is Ecuador's largest city?

Key Words

archaeological: related to the scientific study of human history, often by examining objects

architectural: related to the styles used for designing buildings

Baroque: a style of art and architecture that originated in Europe and was most popular from about 1600 to 1750

biodiversity: the number and variety of species in a geographic region

cabinet: a group of officials who advise a president or other government leader and who often head different departments of the government

cloud forests: tropical forests growing at high altitudes that get much of their water from direct contact with clouds instead of from rain

colonized: claimed and governed by another country

constitution: a written document stating a country's basic principles and laws

dormant: not active for a time

equator: an imaginary circle around Earth's surface that separates the Northern and Southern Hemispheres, or halves, of the planet

hydroelectricity: electricity produced using the energy of moving water, such as in a river

imports: goods a country buys from other countries

Inca Empire: a region covering much of western South America that was ruled by the Inca native peoples during the 1400s and early 1500s

literacy rate: the percentage of a country's population age 15 or older who can read and write

mangroves: trees or shrubs that grow in swamps with salty water and that have roots partly above the ground

monasteries: places where monks, or men in a religious order, live and work

natural selection: a scientific theory describing how living things adapt, or change, over time

panpipe: a wind instrument consisting of pipes of different lengths tied together in a row

plains: flat, treeless areas

plantations: large farms that grow crops to be sold

republic: a form of government in which the head of state is elected

serfs: farm laborers forced to work the land for its owner

tectonic plates: sections of Earth's surface that move very slowly

textiles: woven or knit fabrics and the thread or yarn used to make them

UNESCO: the United Nations Educational, Scientific, and Cultural Organization, whose main goals are to promote world peace and eliminate poverty through education, science,and culture

urban: relating to a city or town

viceroyalty: a region governed by a representative of a king or queen, called a viceroy

Index

Get the best of both worlds.

AV2 bridges the gap between print and digital.

The expandable resources toolbar enables quick access to content including **videos**, **audio**, **activities**, **weblinks**, **slideshows**, **quizzes**, and **key words**.

Animated videos make static images come alive.

Resource icons on each page help readers to further **explore key concepts**.

Published by Lightbox Learning Inc.
276 5th Avenue, Suite 704 #917
New York, NY 10001
Website: www.openlightbox.com

Copyright ©2026 Lightbox Learning Inc.

Library of Congress Control Number: 2024950913

ISBN 979-8-8745-2168-4 (hardcover)
ISBN 979-8-8745-2169-1 (softcover)
ISBN 979-8-8745-2170-7 (static user eBook)
ISBN 979-8-8745-2172-1 (multi-user eBook)

Printed in Guangzhou, China
1 2 3 4 5 6 7 8 9 0 29 28 27 26 25

022025
101324

Project Coordinator: Heather Kissock
Designer: Terry Paulhus
Layout: Mandy Christiansen

Photo Credits
Every reasonable effort has been made to trace ownership and to obtain permission to reprint copyright material. The publisher would be pleased to have any errors or omissions brought to its attention so that they may be corrected in subsequent printings. The publisher acknowledges Getty Images, Alamy, Shutterstock, and Wikimedia Commons as its primary image suppliers for this title.

View new titles and product videos at **www.openlightbox.com**